MEDITATIONS: 21 Days to a Healthier Mind

"Finally, brethren, whatsoever things are true, whatsoever things are honest, whatsoever things are just, whatsoever things are pure, whatsoever things are lovely, whatsoever things are of good report; if there be any virtue, and if there be any praise, think on these things." Phil 4:8, KJV

The next 21 days of your life is going to be an amazing time of healing, clarity and personal breakthrough. We are on a journey to destiny that can often be contaminated by things we experienced; most were unexpected and often traumatic. Fixing your mind requires a cleansing, calibration and consistency. This is the goal of your next 21 days!

I am going to take you on the journey I went through to heal and refocus. I pray this book would help reset your mind so that you can be the best 'you' possible. I believe in you and your ability to conquer every distraction, internally and externally. As we take this journey together, I challenge you to do your best to silence every negative voice in the following 5 areas:

1. Relationships

2. Environments

3. Music

4. TV

5. Social Media

Every sense we have is a gate into our soul. Everything I listed, when unhealthy, can bombard you with negativity that will paralyze your ability to move upward. The things we see, hear, smell, touch and taste leave a residue in our minds that filters into our hearts. We must take control of our "gates" and revoke access to anything that's damaging you. Let's set some criteria for what is going to come into your gates these next 21 days. Let's create two folders (Positive and Negative). Assign everything you do: relationships, environments, songs, TV shows and social media to a mental folder. It can only stay in the POSITIVE folder if it:

1. Adds holistic value to your life (Mind, Body and Soul)

2. Contributes to helping you accomplish your destiny

3. Helps to eliminate negative thoughts of unbelief, fear and apprehension

Put anything that **does not** meet the criteria into the NEGATIVE folder. We are applying this principle to the food we eat as well. The mouth is a gate that leads to a lot of our unhappiness, sickness and disease. Eat lots of fresh fruits, vegetables and lean grilled meats; nothing processed which includes fast food or junk food. Make the next 21 days a complete cleanse and recalibration.

For the best results, make the effort to guard every gate for the next 21 days so we can work together and create the best environment possible for healing, clarity and personal breakthrough in your life.

5. **LOVELY**
DAY 13: PAST:
It Wasn't All Bad Psalms 37:25
DAY 14: PRESENT:
Great Things Are Happening RIGHT NOW
Jeremiah 29:11
DAY 15: FUTURE:
My Future Is Bright 1 Corinthians 2:9

6. **THE GOOD REPORT**
DAY 16: PAST:
It Couldn't Kill Me Philippians 1:6
DAY 17: PRESENT:
I'm Still Here Daniel 3:27
Day 18: FUTURE:
I'll Always Survive Psalms 34:19

7. **FORWARD MEDITATIONS**
DAY 19: PAST:
I Always Wanted To _____ Genesis 37:5
DAY 20: PRESENT:
The Dreams That Won't Die Habakkuk 2:2
DAY 21: FUTURE:
BELIEVE! Luke: 8:50

SECTION 1: TRUTH

DAY 1: PAST: **It Was Necessary. Romans 8:28**

I was a personal trainer for 7 years and was always amazed at the intolerance clients often showed for the process required to meet their goal. Clients possess goals while trainers provide plans by which they can be accomplished. You solicit a trainer for weight loss or strength training because *your* process has not been working and you need new information to get to your desired achievement. The jubilation that comes from accomplishment is a byproduct of the pain and sacrifice you made to meet your objective. When you arrive at destiny, the pain experienced on the way becomes a distant memory.

The past was necessary for the strength and wisdom we have presently. Embrace what happened as a catalyst for what will be. Have faith that the catalyst, no matter how painful, created some characteristics in you necessary to accomplish destiny. Though it feels unbearable at the time, it works for our good in the future.

Life Application: Identify 3 events in your past that were painful or traumatic. Then, write five characteristics you gained from each which you feel contributed to who you are today. Now, ask yourself, how can the lessons you learned from each event assist you in reaching your destiny? In the future, make a conscious effort to clearly identify the trauma and pull the positive from each event to help propel you toward your goals.

DAY 2: PRESENT: I'm Growing. 1 Peter 2:1-2

We are growing and changing at this very moment. Our teenage years were an awkward time for most of us because we found that growth could not be predicted. Teeth sometimes grew faster than the mouth and feet often grew faster than the legs. Compared to the magazine photos of my athletic heroes, I felt like I would never measure up. After I started working out, I never looked like what I saw in my head. Most of us look back on our teenage school pictures with some sense of embarrassment because they are tangible evidence of the awkward stages. Some of those experiences stayed with us through the years but we kept nourishing, eating and growing until our bodies matured.

Pain is not always the result of being attacked, but rather the evidence that we are being stretched. Our bones and muscles are growing to help us become mature vessels by which our destiny can be accomplished. The frustration we often experience is the disparity between where we are and how we envision ourselves in the future. Embrace the awkward places and understand you are changing and transforming into a mature vessel equipped for purpose.

Life Application: Identify at least five areas in which you were "pushed" out of your comfort zone. Although it may have hurt or made you feel uncomfortable, in what ways have you grown and how can that growth assist you in reaching your goals?

DAY 3: FUTURE: It's Possible. Mark 9:23

At some point, we stopped being the child full of dreams and ideas. Survival settled us into a rustic reality where dreams are unattainable figments of our imagination. As elementary school kids, we used to relish the question: "What do you want to be when you grow up?" Hands would violently fly into the air accompanied by grunts and weird noises. Every child possessed an eager desire to share without any inhibition. What happened to us?

At some point, we stopped believing that those extravagant dreams were possible. Anything is possible if we believe. Calamity should not change our reality. I found I was unhappy when I allowed my dreams to give way to unfavorable circumstances. Peter walked on water in the midst of a storm. Stop waiting on the ideal situation to do miraculous things. Allow faith to guide your belief during unfavorable times. You are never too young or old to begin. Every day you wake up is another opportunity to dream, create, build and invent. Make a promise to yourself that you will not waste another opportunity but will seize each moment to destroy the roadblocks you have encountered. Take control of your life and allow yourself to live, laugh, love and DREAM AGAIN! It is possible.

Life Application: Do you remember your dreams? What are they? Make a list of those things that have caused you to deny yourself from accomplishing your dreams? Now, identify steps to overcome each obstacle in order to reach your goal.

SECTION 2: HONESTY

DAY 4: PAST: Self Inflicted. Matthew 7:20

Mom would always warn us about a hot oven as kids. From those experiences, I discovered three kinds of people. *Oven watchers* can read the oven dial and tell that it's hot. *Oven testers* must get close enough to feel the heat of the oven before acknowledging that it's hot. *Oven touchers* won't learn it's hot until they actually touch it and get burned. All three types of people will learn the same lesson but one group is left with scars...Self-inflicted scars.

Great freedom comes when we mature enough to acknowledge we created the perfect environment for many of the difficult, horrific things we experienced. We didn't obey the stop signs and we ignored every clue that the situation was all bad. It may have been a relationship, business decision or a legal matter. We foolishly volunteered for some of the most ridiculous things that happened in our past and it left us scarred. Before we blame externally, look internally. Accept responsibility for when you needed to touch the oven. It will free you and cause you to redirect some forgiveness inwardly.

Life Application: What type of person are you...an oven watcher, oven tester or oven toucher? Be honest with your self-identification and identify ways in which you may have inflicted your own scars. List 3 things you can do differently in the future to prevent unnecessary pain you may have inflicted upon yourself in the past.

DAY 5: PRESENT: I Could Do More.
Proverbs 12:4

I had the skill to make my high school varsity basketball team but the coach told my dad I was too skinny. I had to embrace the fact that I had not done enough to get me to my next goal. There was an area of my development that I omitted. Success at new levels requires greater sacrifice. I had to *do* more to *be* more.

Maturity demands a willingness to embrace the new information required to go to the next place of success. Frustration sets in when we start feeling stagnant but it could be an indication that we need new information. What was hard work and admirable in middle school is laziness in college. New levels require new commitments, information and sacrifice. The grind grows as we grow. Living from old success is no longer an option. Embrace newness and develop the areas you omitted.

Life Application: Examine your goals today. Are you doing everything possible to approach destiny? If not, what more can you do? Are you accessing and open to the new information necessary to push you forward? Are you applying the new information or just "collecting" it?

DAY 6: FUTURE: Fear Will Never Stop Me Again. 2 Timothy 1:7

I remember being on the bus as a 3rd grader listening to the 4th graders tell me how difficult their grade was and how easy 3rd grade was. They cited mean teachers, unbearable homework and a classwork load that could not be put into words. A subtle fear would grip my heart as I kept listening to the older kids render a slow verbal death to everyone on the bus. The following year, I walked into 4th grade with a subtle tremble in my new white shoes (that would be beige by days end) only to find out it wasn't that bad. Mrs. Banks was the same teddy bear teacher, full of love and smiles, that my teacher was last year. It was all hype, but the kids did the same thing every year and the pattern continued into adulthood. Driving, college, dating, marriage, bills, kids, employment, leadership, ministry, business and so on. People seek to make you afraid where they may have failed.

God gave us everything we needed to be what He wanted. The instruction we receive on one level equips us for the next. Embrace new levels knowing that you will figure this out. We may not have all the details, but we must maintain an absence of fear and a presence of power. God would never allow you to walk into a new place unprepared. Take dominion and never let that fear grip you again.

Life Application: What are you afraid of? Be specific and honest with yourself. List each fear and the reason it exists. Can you see yourself overcoming these "obstacles"? Are the things listed worth forfeiting your dreams and goals?

SECTION 3: JUST
DAY 7: PAST: Let It Go! Philippians 3:13-14

I was playing basketball at a team camp held at the Atlanta Hawks' facility when I collided knee to knee with a 7'2 center ! My leg went numb and I heard the crowd go silent and I knew something was wrong. My tournament was done. After the doctor used 4 large needles to drain it, he explained the knee dislocated, but no surgery was required. I had months of extensive rehab and a huge knee brace to wear to be ready for the start of the next season. When I could play again, I continued to wear the brace and my mind constantly went back to the last time I was hurt. Our team trainer looked at me one day and said 'you don't need that thing anymore'. I told him it made me feel better and he said: "Your knee will never heal to its original strength as long as you keep wearing that brace. Take it off..."

Oftentimes we heal, but we mentally relive the horrific experiences that caused the original injury. We cannot look back and run forward. We keep the brace on because we 'think' ourselves insulated from experiencing the same trauma again. Our minds can be locked in a place where the body no longer exists. You can always tell your mental location based on your current conversations. Remember the lesson but forget the calamity. It happened, but it doesn't hurt anymore. You don't need the brace. Let it go!

Life Application: What has been your "pattern" of coping when dealing with trauma? If constantly thinking on past hurts hindered your forward movement, what steps can you take to LET IT GO?

DAY 8: PRESENT: Forgive! Matt. 6:14-15

Running track requires you to be as light as possible. Every extra ounce can potentially add to your time and hinder your ability to win the race. You also have to watch your food intake and ensure that you are getting the nutrients necessary to keep your body operating at optimal levels. A weighted down runner is only unrealized potential. Are you weighted?

Life is a race of endurance. Unforgiveness is a heavy garment and a hindrance to our ability to run at the right pace. We sacrifice our peace when we hold on to our past. Running from forgiveness will manifest itself through frustrations, anger, bitterness and oftentimes illness. Don't wait until it doesn't hurt. Forgiveness is the choice Jesus made at the height of His suffering on the cross and He didn't wait for an apology. Waiting on people to recognize the gravity of the pain they caused is a waste of our time. We put our lives on pause privately demanding something from people that showed us they are either oblivious or don't care. RELEASE YOURSELF through forgiveness. If possible, have the conversations you need to have but by all means, take the steps necessary to release people that hurt you as you desire to live life freely. Cultivate a life where you can daily release the people that hurt you. It's a lot of work holding a weight while trying to win a race.

Life Application: Examine areas in your life where you have been hurt, betrayed or traumatized in some way. How did you handle it? Are you waiting on closure that may never come? What steps can you take to move forward?

DAY 9: FUTURE: God Will Reward Me (in this life). Psalms 27:13

Heaven was talked about a lot in my childhood. We want to make heaven our home. I remember reading the bible stories of our patriarchs as a child and realizing: They did some awesome things in this life, too. I loved reading about King Solomon and his wisdom. He used the best to build God's temple. His wealth was well known and the Queen of Sheba traveled months to be in his presence. His wealth led to his witness. Healthy, wealthy and wise.

Holistic prosperity is God's plan for us. Our marriages, families, finances, health and businesses should prosper. When we connect to God, we are seated with Him in heavenly places on a daily basis. We will see miracles and manifestation of His presence in this earth. As we do our part, He will show up in every situation and His presence demands transformation. At some point in my healing process, I had to stop delaying my expectations for great things. Expectation breeds results. As you heal, your heart opens again. We often lose hope because someone let us down or fell short of our expectations but God never fails. God has plans that faith will manifest. Faith creates an atmosphere for God to move. Give faith access to every area of your life today!

Life Application: Have you lowered your expectations based on past hurts or disappointments? If so, why? Make an effort to spend more time with God on a daily basis. As you begin to refocus and rediscover Him intimately, make a list of your new expectations moving forward.

SECTION 4: PURE

DAY 10: PAST: What poisoned me? Ephesians 4:31

I've had about 7 bouts with food poisoning and at the onset of symptoms, the first question you ask is: "What did I eat?" As your body exhibits rebellious behaviors that are beyond your control, a severe poisoning makes one question if their existence should continue. What poisoned you?

Do you ever find that you want to stop doing something or thinking in a manner that seems involuntary? Nasty, rude and unappealing behaviors or thought processes can often be on auto pilot. We have all ingested information or modeled a behavior that wasn't good for us. Many cycles form from a time where our environment was unhealthy or our situation was rooted in desperation, survival or war. Emerging from difficult times can often leave the mind poisoned and perceptions flawed. Unfortunately, when life skills are learned from unhealthy people, unfruitful thought processes and behaviors become an integral part of our being. It takes strength to admit weakness so we must acknowledge areas of our mind and heart that are infected. You have a lot to do with how people see you. When you see cycles of failure, it could be connected to poison.

Life Application: Write down areas in which you are unhealthy and what influenced the unhealthy mindset or behavior? THAT was the poison! It's time for recalibration. In your study time, compare your list with the characteristics of God. If it's not found in the Bible, get rid of it! Write steps that will help you shed the old and walk in the new!

_____

DAY 11: PRESENT: Am I Still Contaminated?
Galatians 5:22

Gastroparesis? It is literally a paralyzed stomach...and I had it. I actually contracted post-viral gastro paresis which meant that as a result of the stomach virus I was now free of; I was suffering from another condition that meant my digestive system stopped working. Wonderful! For 30 days, I was unable to eat solids. I would feel as if I had eaten from a buffet after just two sips of water. I slept sitting up, miserable, constantly bloated, in pain, perpetually nauseous and experiencing some of the same limitations I had when I had the stomach virus only...I didn't.

Recovering from poison is not an overnight process and though you may be free from the contaminants, there are often residual effects that still have to be dealt with. This becomes evident in trust issues and unwarranted suspiciousness of people that mean you well. If we are so focused on what hurt us in the past, we will miss what is presently in our life to heal us. Don't be afraid to change what's not working for you. Newness brings joy so open up and allow the last bit of contamination out so that you can be completely free to embrace newness.

Life Application: So, you made a plan and wrote steps to accomplish it...great! Now what? Let's identify the "issues" and defensive behaviors you have developed due to the trauma experienced. These behaviors seemed like the best solution to protect yourself from being hurt again. Once identified, make an effort to take small steps toward complete healing by altering your mindset as you continue to grow in God.

DAY 12: FUTURE: Staying Free. Galatians 5:1
Age brings dietary limitations. "When you get older, you won't be able to eat that!" my dad used to say laughingly. After I rebutted he would say: "Ok, you'll see buddy" He was right. The foolish things I used to ingest are no longer welcomed by my digestive system. I am at peace with it because it forces me to make healthier decisions to stay free of disease and maintain control of my body. Maturity brings a greater desire for freedom.

Forgiveness is an essential part of staying free, but it doesn't mean that you allow the same access to the people and relationships that damaged you. Dysfunctional people must be loved from a distance, so never feel guilty about cutting unhealthy relationships. Stay free of the environments, relationships and affiliations that contributed to your past failures. Set boundaries because you are carrying precious cargo: Destiny. Hurt people will always hurt people. You may have been too emotional to recognize how hurt they really were which is a mistake we all make. Don't assume that people were aware of how they damaged you. Jesus was on the cross and said: *"Father, forgive them; for they do not know what they are doing."*

Life Application: When you make progress, what seems to take you two steps back? An addiction, a relationship, family, etc.? Identify the cause and omit it from your life. Protect your destiny by changing your environments and conversations. If you find it difficult to do this yourself, speak with a counselor who can help. Have the courage to make changes!

SECTION 5: LOVELY

DAY 13: PAST: It Wasn't All Bad. Psalms 37:25

Objects in mirror are closer than they appear. Dad would take us on long road trips and I used to look at it on the side mirrors of the car all the time when I was kid. I would slip into these long gazes watching the trees go by at rapid pace because dad was a chronic speeder. I never understood that phrase on the mirrors until I was able to drive. Mirrors provide inaccurate reflections and there are often blind spots.

Reflecting on the past can often present a skewed view of the way things happened. We perceive the world through a lens that is not always accurate. God uses life as the ultimate teacher and there will be victories and trophies to remind us of how lovely life can be when we pass the test. We often focus on our failures too much and become too critical of experiences that taught us essential lessons. God has never forsaken us, but he may seem quiet at points. When God is quiet, remember you are being tested. Test Day. The room was silent and the teacher was different. The warmth they had when teaching turned to a cold silence as the test was placed face down on your desk. God is often the same way. Quietly watching if we will apply the lessons he taught us through our past.

Life Application: Have you felt "ignored" by God? In retrospect, was it a test? Did you pass or does it seem so keep coming back around? Think on a specific event where it seemed like you were stuck in a cycle. Identify the test, use wisdom you've gained through experience and apply the new information learned to release yourself from the cycle.

DAY 14: PRESENT: Great Things Are Happening RIGHT NOW. Jeremiah 29:11

FRUSTRATED! The wife and I made plans to do these awesome things for the kids but they messed up royally this time. The standards of our home are clearly communicated. Love God, Love Each other, work hard in school and complete your chores. If these four things are completed, they can ask for anything.... almost anything. Report cards come home and they are less than what we are accustomed to seeing. We don't fuss or yell, but we ask questions. The answers are even less stellar. You didn't fail because you couldn't succeed, you failed because you didn't turn in homework and then you didn't turn in CLASSWORK? Plans delayed.

A good parent never rewards bad behavior because it spoils the child and creates a sense of entitlement. The Bible is full of the if/then principle. God is making plans for us right now, but He wants us to walk in a level of maturity that will allow us to handle the blessings properly. When there are delays, it's not always a plot of the enemy to derail our blessings, neither is it that we are waiting on God. Many times, He's waiting on us. Like children, we often ask for new things when we haven't obeyed old instructions. Great things are happening RIGHT NOW, but we must be positioned in obedience to receive them.

Life Application: Have you been obedient to God in all areas of your life? If not, why? How can you avoid the frustration of feeling like you're not making progress? List the steps to accomplish this goal.

DAY 15: FUTURE: My Future Is Bright. 1
Corinthians 2:9

Christmas was always special. Dad got more excited
about Christmas than we did. One year, we woke up to
him falling down the stairs as he rushed to get his
horribly wrapped gifts under the tree. Becoming a
parent helped me understand. There is a special joy that
comes with seeing a look of surprise on the faces of the
people you love. Dad would always get mom something
that made her cry. He taught me to listen year round,
plan and research so the surprise would be paramount!
I'm always listening to my wife and kids. I watch how
they respond to everything because it reveals their
interests. I file it knowing one day I'll have the ability
and the opportunity to get it.

God hears, sees and knows everything. He created us
with the desires that we have. He is passionate about
utilizing the rest of our lives to bless and prosper us as
we draw closer to him. The pursuit of God creates an
atmosphere that tailors your desires to His heart. I
know what my wife needs and likes because there is
relationship so I do before she asks. When I see she
needs it, I seek to exceed her need. Love doesn't wait
for an occasion; it creates an occasion. Your future is
full of those 'just because' moments. Embrace God
more today knowing he's thinking of ways to blow your
mind.

Life Application: Are you as close to God as you can
be or has life takes precedence over your personal time
with Him? Make an appointment with God and don't
cancel! Designate time each day that belongs to God
for prayer, worship and study.

SECTION 6: THE GOOD REPORT

DAY 16: PAST: It Couldn't Kill Me. Philippians 1:6

7th Grade basketball tryouts and we haven't touched a ball! 40 degrees outside and we are in our basketball shorts and cutoff t-shirts. We ran outside from the middle school to the high school, all the stadium stairs, hills, and a mile to finish it off for the first 4 days! Hundreds of kids showed up the first day. By day 5, we were down to about 40 and the final cut was 15.

We often look for our trials to make sense. Our minds seek understanding from the obscurity of life's storms. We have to remember that trials aren't sent to us, but entrusted to us. It cannot kill you because you were created to overcome it. It was designed to strengthen you, but not to destroy you. Your trials will expose the giant in you and the character of the people around you (see Job). Stop looking at your difficulties as the end but rather the beginning of what's next. The struggles you are feeling right now are temporary tests that will prepare you for long term success. You are going to make the team. Hang in there. GO GET IT!

Life Application: Identify three of the biggest trials you have faced. What did you learn from each and how did it make you stronger? As you move forward, learn to embrace your storm knowing that when it's over, you'll be better, stronger and wiser. Share your testimony to encourage others and walk in confidence knowing you were chosen to win!

DAY 17: PRESENT: I'm Still Here. Daniel 3:27

When I was in it, I never saw myself getting beyond it. The car accident did nerve damage to the left side of my body and I went from being a scholarship athlete to a student working his way through school. Depressed, frustrated, irritated and feeling like my faith failed me; I was in this dark place where everything I worked for had suddenly disappeared.

When you look back on your life, you find many instances in which you survived. You may not have won a battle in warrior-like fashion but you outlasted what was trying to kill you. You went into the fire and the fire couldn't burn you. Today, let's look back on those victories that took a lasting faith. We are so used to fighting things off or escaping an oncoming threat, but sometimes you have to embrace the endurance races. Some things required us to just stand still and see the salvation of God operate on our behalf. Looking down the barrel of a gun that can't shoot you. Standing in a room of gas that doesn't affect you. Walking in a lightning storm that doesn't strike you. God often places us in hazardous environments mentally, physically, emotionally and spiritually to show that in our fragileness, he still preserves us. You're still here.

Life Application: What was it that tried to "kill" you, figuratively or literally? Was it a relationship, an illness or something else? How did God show up in that situation? While the negative will be there to "push" you, always make an effort to meditate on the positive that came from that situation and the fact that God wouldn't allow it to take you out. You're…still…here.

Day 18: FUTURE: I'll Always Survive. **Psalms 34:19**
Naysayers present themselves at every phase of life.
They say things like: "when you do this, for this amount
of time, then you will experience this new thing that will
really knock your socks off because you have no idea
what's in store for you because I am way more
experienced and traumatized and you too will
experience the same trauma because I'm special as the
result of the trauma I experienced.....and you're
naïve...so there...I told you"

The reality is: God always causes us to triumph when
we seek Him. Those same people that promote fear
have often hit difficulties because they were doing life
without His guidance. Look back on your life and you
understand that you jumped every hurdle. You hit some
of them, but you got over them. Everything people said
to try to instill fear about the 2nd grade, graduation,
driving, marriage or starting a business was, in large
part, their own tarnished experiences based on skewed
data. You can do anything you prepare yourself to do.
We must learn to shut out the doubters that instill fear.
2nd grade was awesome, graduation was a blast, been
driving for years, marriage is a beautiful thing and
businesses are good! You'll survive every challenge and
discover the champion in you as you always have. Quiet
the voices that feed your fear and aggressively meet
every obstacle in front of you. You've got this!

Life Application: Who or what are the negative voices
you always seem to encounter? Do you listen? If so,
why? What differences can you make to silence the
negativity in the midst of your progress?

SECTION 7: FORWARD MEDITATIONS

DAY 19: PAST: I Always Wanted To ____.
Genesis 37:5

The room was full of anxious youngsters in the 1st grade. I was the substitute teacher and I love kids so I was excited to do it. I asked the infamous question to a few. "What do you want to be when you grow up?" The excitement in their eyes was contagious as they reflected on vivid dreams of splendor and success. There was no shortage of ambition or aspiration.

It's time for you to start again but that often means going back to the beginning. Go back to the place where you didn't care what people thought. Return to the youthful confidence exhibited when asked what you wanted from life. Fear is a learned behavior and a contagious disease that limits upward movement. Today, we are committing to move beyond internal limitations in pursuit of our original destiny. We were created for purpose and it is time to dream again and discover what that purpose is. Get out of your own way and dream the dream. Dream it again and then position yourself to carry out the dream. Share it with the right people that have been where you are going and keep it from the naysayers. What is the dream(s) that you never stopped dreaming? Dreams are sneak peeks of coming attractions! Don't let it die; the world needs the dream inside of you. Let it out!

Life Application: Reflect on dreams then and now. Are you still excited? If not, why? Have you gained the courage to embrace your dream(s)? Have you taken steps to achieve them? If not, why?

DAY 20: PRESENT: The Dreams That Won't Die.
Habakkuk 2:2

It's not real until you write it. The dream was given to you but if it's just for you, it's too small. The dream is connected to a people, a community, a nation or a world. You have to write so that others can read it and run with it. If you are thinking you can do it by yourself, you have already failed. You need the right people around you to push it forward. You can trust now because you have the right perception of the world around you. You are healthy enough to recognize healthy relationships and you are poised to make big moves NOW. When it's a God-given dream, it never dies. Dreams become vision and vision becomes reality based on one act of faith. Write it!

Somebody is waiting on you to pursue what you saw in your dreams. The void that you feel internally was placed by God because there is a void in the earth. Your dream is a solution to a problem, but don't miss your window. If you don't use it, you'll look up one day and see that someone else has put your dream in action. This happens because the earth needed the solution. Prayer connects you to a line of communication where solutions are constantly being downloaded. You can log on as others can. When we pray to God, we tap in to our Source who is full of witty inventions, ideas and innovations that the earth needs. You have access to solutions that you have not used. Your time is NOW!

Life Application: Were you given vision by God for a business, invention or other solution that keeps coming back to you? Write a plan and write steps to destroy your excuses and bring your vision to pass!

24

DAY 21: FUTURE: **BELIEVE! Luke: 8:50**
At the conclusion of our journey together, I pray for your ability to simply BELIEVE. Believe in God, believe in you, and believe in your future. Believe in the people that God places in your life. Your spouse, your employees, your team…Hold on to your ability to believe in the face of ever-present adversity and difficulties. Storms will come but you will continue to believe. Peter walked on water in the midst of a storm. Don't wait for a favorable time to exercise your faith. Your faith activates the "water-walker" in you.
We often focus on the fact that Peter sank, but forget that he walked towards Jesus. When he sank he cried for help and Jesus helped him. Here is the amazing thing about the conclusion of the event: If Peter walked out to Jesus, how did he get back to the boat? When your faith fails, ask for help but never forget you are still a water-walker. The moment you start believing again, you become the water-walker you were supposed to be. The storms are just a distraction but they can't kill you. Stay focused; believe at all times because all things are possible. ONLY BELIEVE!

Life Application: Go back and review each day we have spent together and read your responses to the questions. Do you see your growth? Has your mindset changed? How? Keep this book as a handy reference to help you refocus on life's journey and to remind you of what you are capable of if you only believe.

www.ingramcontent.com/pod-product-compliance
Lightning Source LLC
Chambersburg PA
CBHW071450040426
42445CB00012BA/1505